This book belongs to

Mommy

and

_____

(my name)

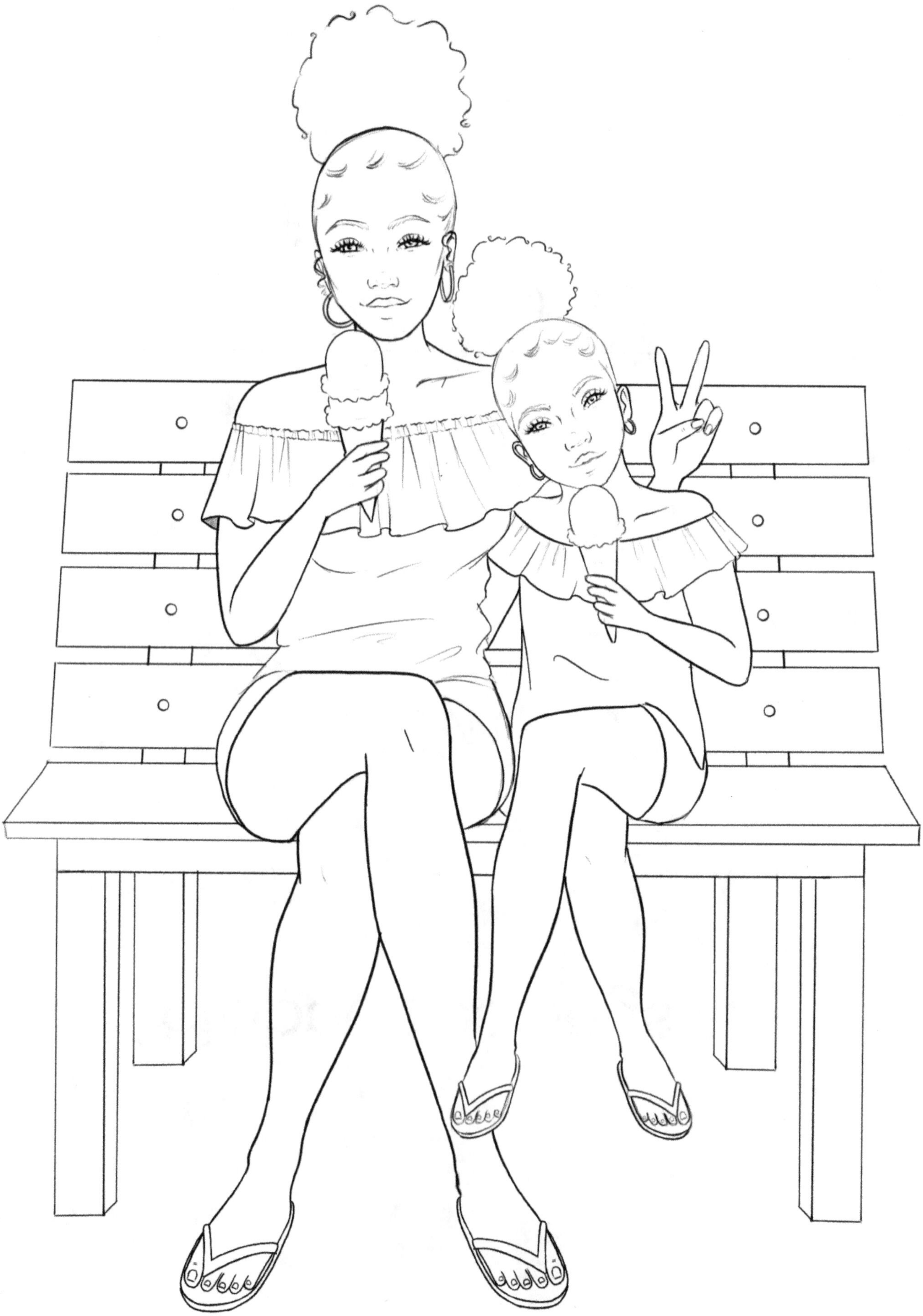

Mommy’s Side

My Side

My Side

My Side

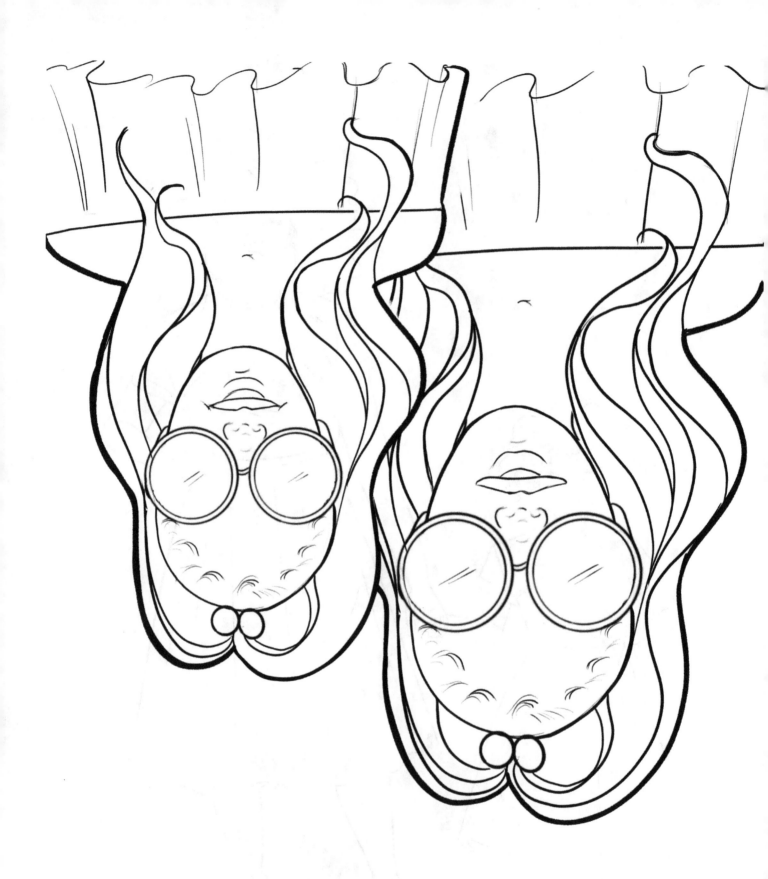

My Side

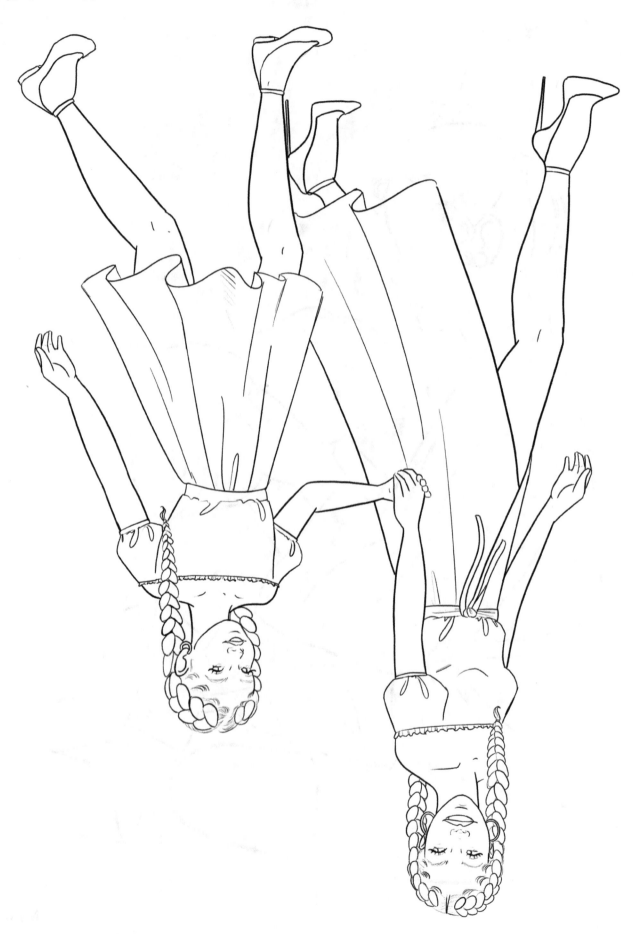

My Side

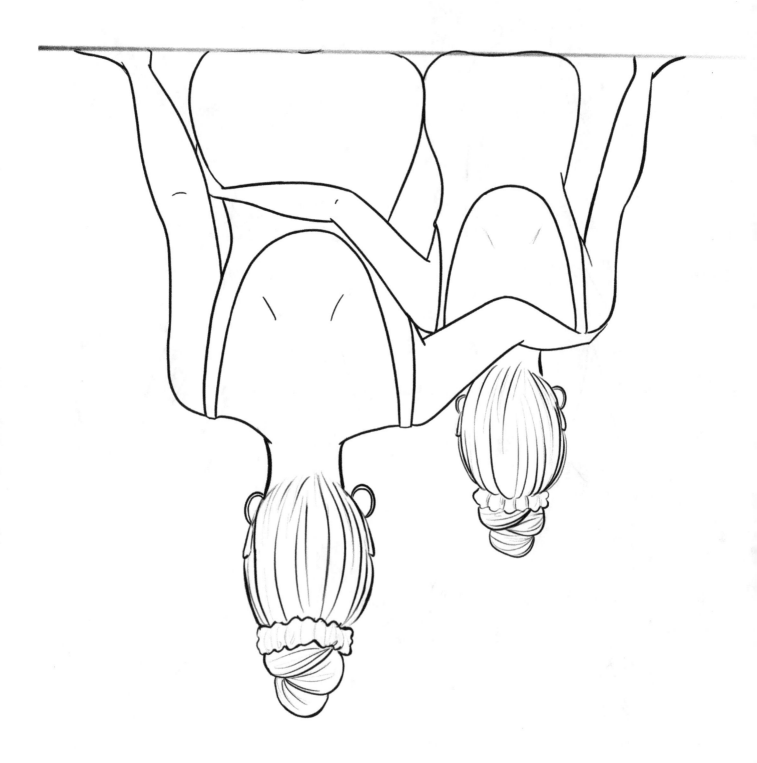

My Side

My Side

My Side

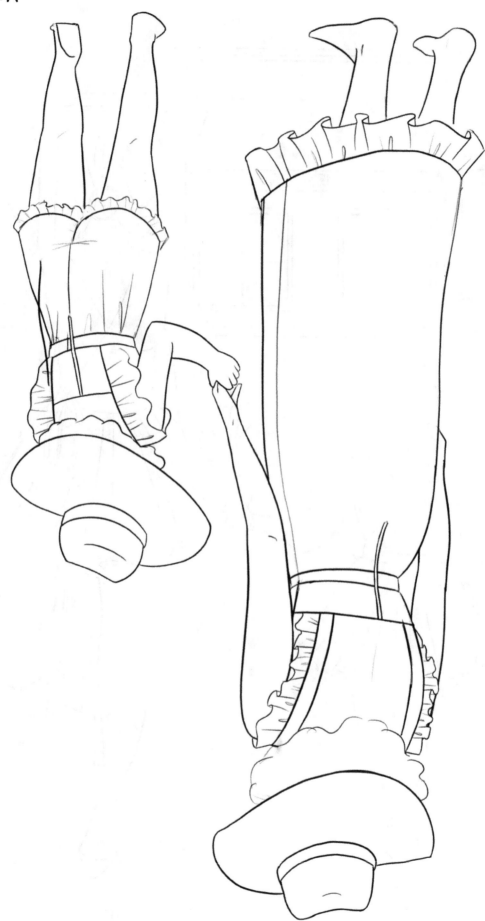

My Side

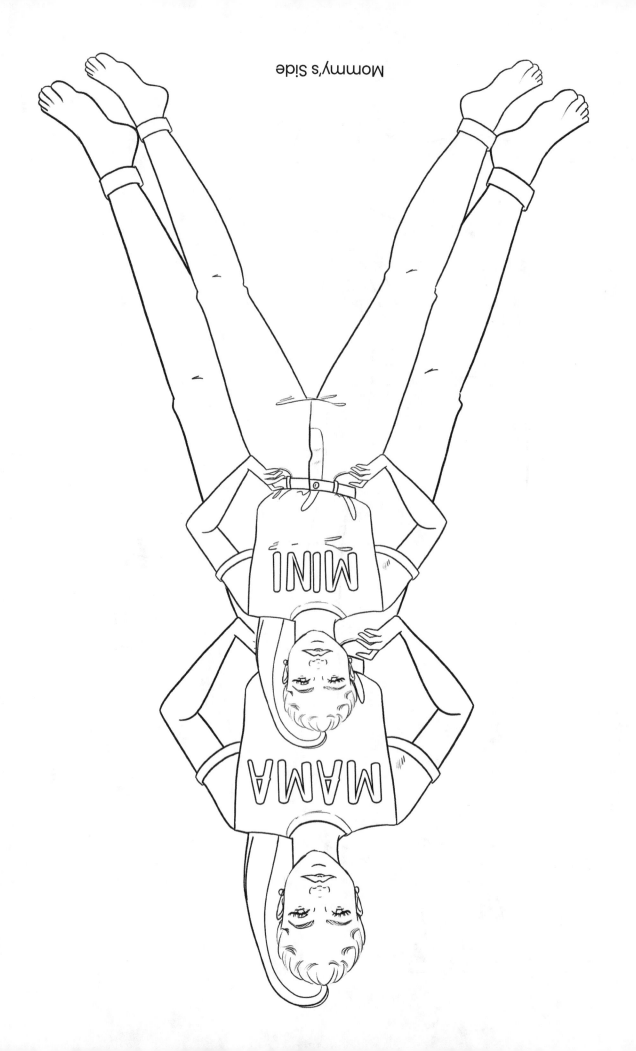

My Side

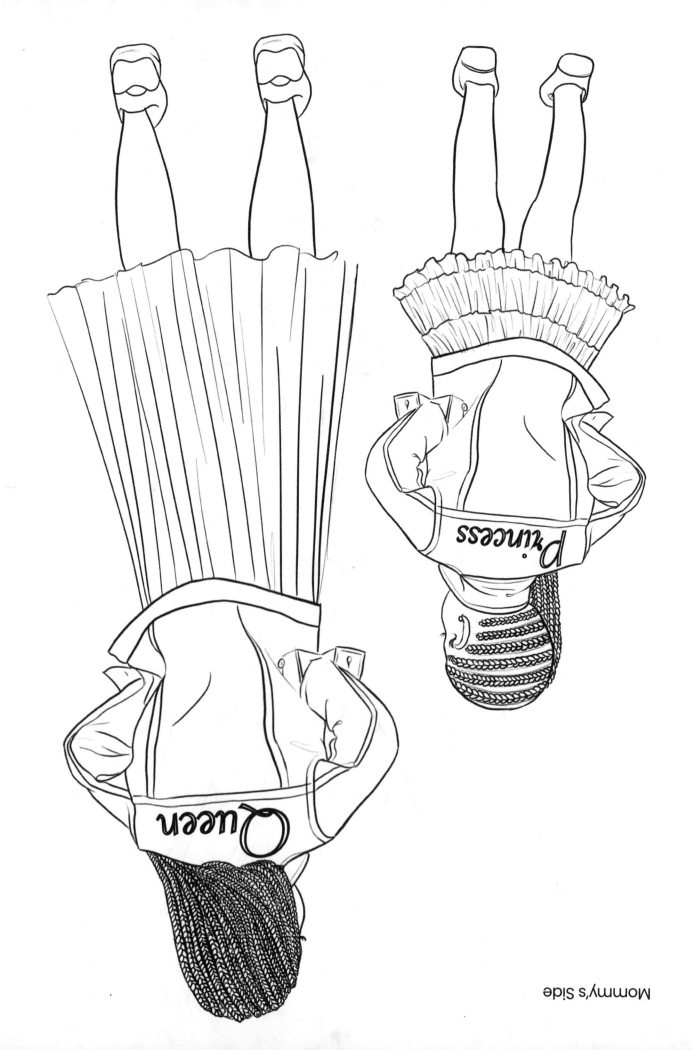

My Side

My Side

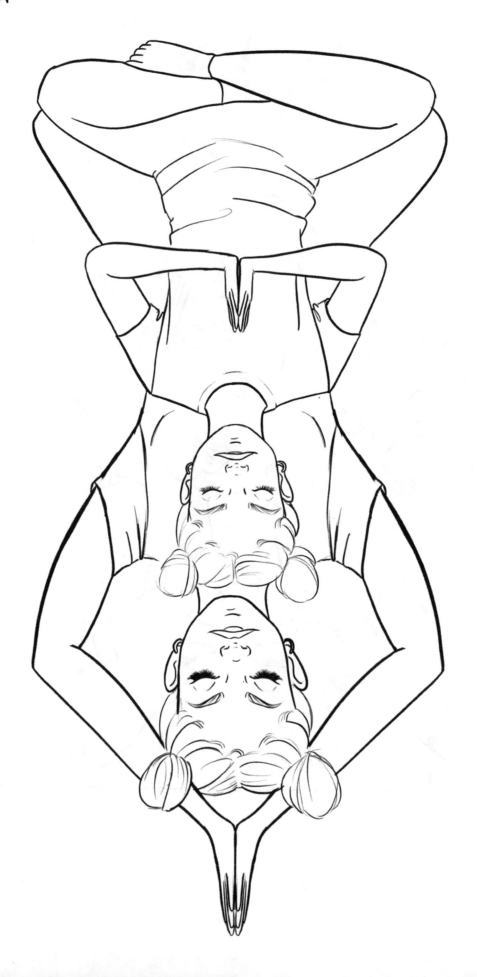

My Side

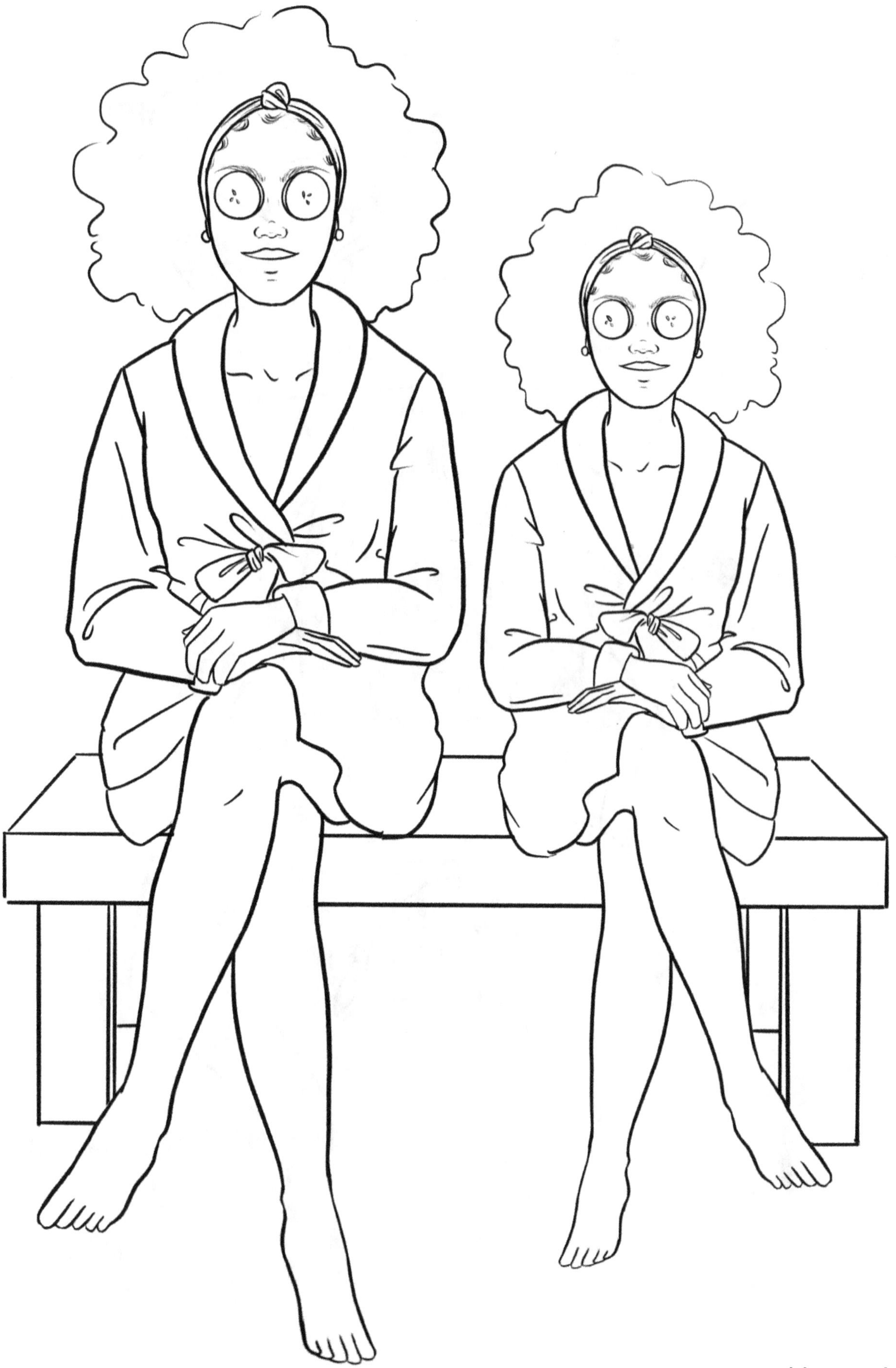

My Side

My Side

My Side

My Side

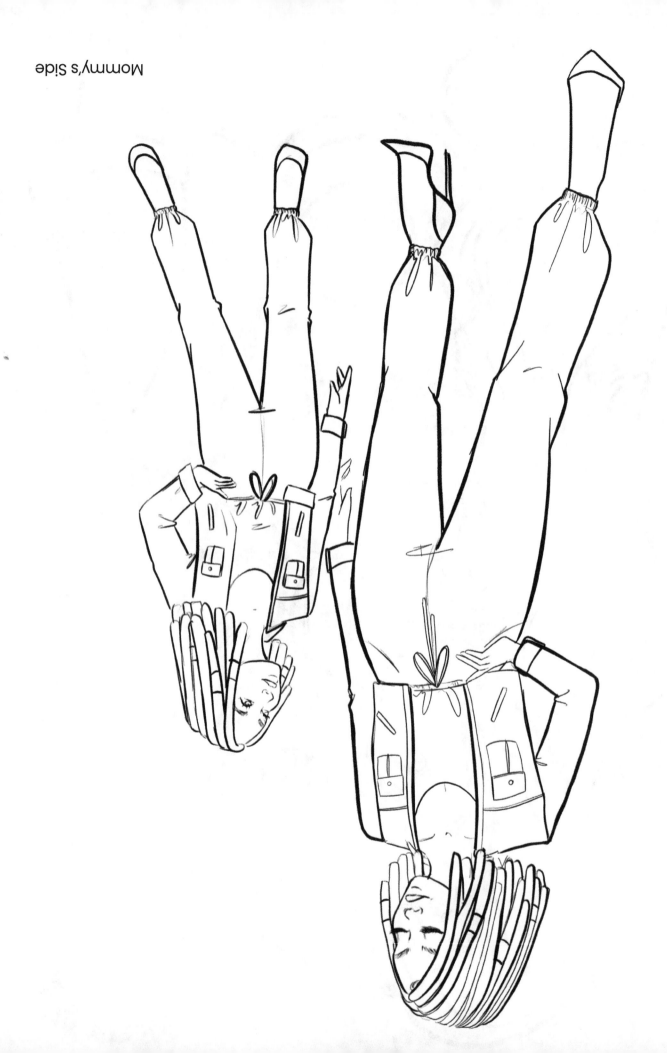

My Side

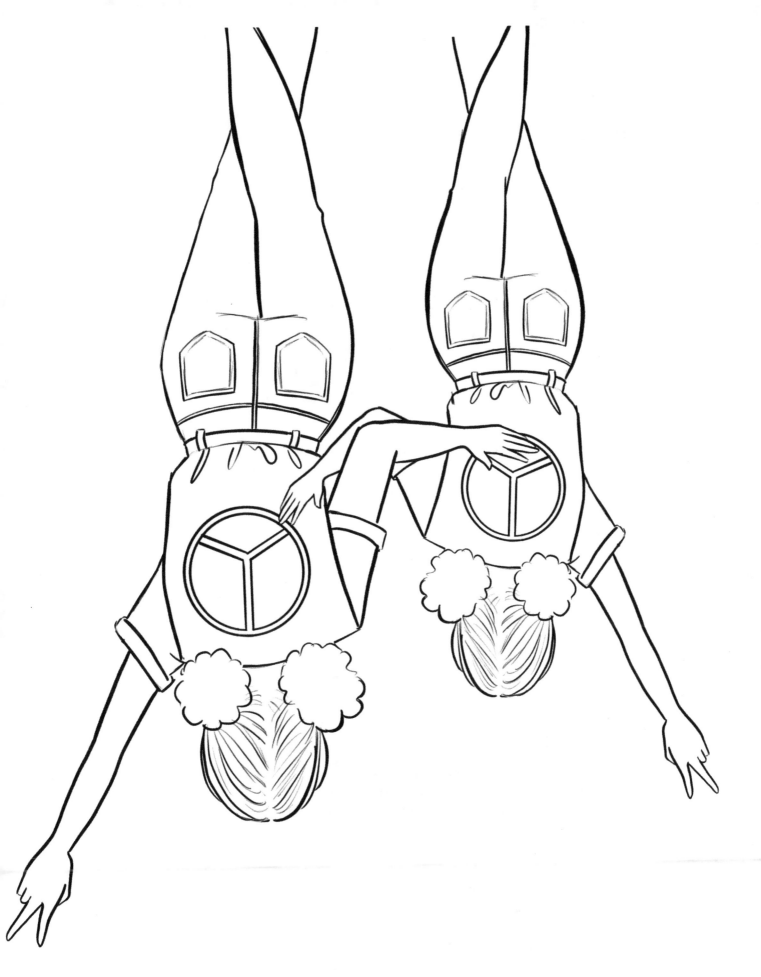

My Side

Printed in the United States of America
First Printing, 2020
ISBN: 978-0-578-73821-5

Bre'Anda Conwell is an entrepreneur and author who was born and raised in the small town of Bessemer, Alabama. She attended the HBCU Miles College and graduated with honors and a bachelor's degree in Business Administration. Since leaving college Bre'Anda has put her entrepreneurial skills to good use. She became the Founder and CEO of Conwell Publishing. A company whose mission is to educate and inspire children and adults alike on how to self publish, market and sell their own novels. Bre'Anda's books include coloring books, journals, and many more to come.

For More about Bre'anda, visit her website at www.breconwell.com or like her facebook fan page at www.facebook.com/breconwell

Conwell Publishing, LLC

Suite 500
1601 5th Ave North
Birmingham, Al 35203
www.breconwell.com

CPSIA information can be obtained
at www.ICGtesting.com
Printed in the USA
BVHW090533130920
588369BV00004B/347